THE BATTLE OF THE

VIRTUES
& VICES

THE BATTLE OF THE

VIRTUES

& VICES

DEFENDING THE INTERIOR CASTLE OF THE SOUL

POPE SAINT LEO IX

TRANSLATED BY
FR. ROBERT NIXON, OSB

TAN Books

Gastonia, North Carolina

Translated by Fr. Robert Nixon, OSB

Cover design by Jordan Avery

Cover image credit: *St. Michael* by Luca Giordano, circa 1663, oil on canvas. Image is in Public Domain via Wikimedia Commons.

ISBN: 978-1-5051-3174-1
Kindle ISBN: 978-1-5051-3184-0
ePUB ISBN: 978-1-5051-3185-7

Published in the United States by
TAN Books
PO Box 269
Gastonia, NC 28053
www.TANBooks.com

Printed in the United States of America

"To the one who is victorious, I shall grant to sit upon My throne with Me; just as I was victorious, and sit with My Father in His throne."

—Revelation 3:21

Contents

TRANSLATOR'S NOTE

THE BATTLE BETWEEN the virtues and the vices is a real part of every person's life, regardless of age, gender, or state in life (with the singular exceptions of Jesus Christ Himself and the Blessed Virgin Mary). For a tendency to sin, as well as a natural desire for the good, are both intrinsic parts of our mortal human nature. The tendency to sin arises from the primordial fall of Adam and Eve, which has given rise to innumerable deficiencies and defects in our character and nature. The opposing tendency—the desire for that which is truly good—emerges both from the innate dignity of our condition as creatures fashioned in the image and likeness of God and by virtue of the grace bestowed upon us through Our Lord Jesus Christ.

These opposing tendencies in our nature often confront each other headlong, almost in a kind of battle for dominance over the soul. This battle between the virtues and vices is the theme of the present work, which depicts this interior struggle between good and evil in the form of a dialogue between various vices and the virtues which serve to oppose them.

The Latin original of this dialogue (or series of dialogues) was one of the most popular and widely circulated works in the latter portion of the Middle Ages, and a great multitude of manuscript copies of it exist. Not surprisingly for such a widely circulated and copied work, the various manuscript versions of it exhibit numerous small differences, perhaps reflecting particular insights or redactional choices of the individual copyists. The identification of the author is also extremely variable. Some manuscripts give the author as Saint Ambrose of Milan (c. 339–397), while others attribute it to the pen of Saint Leo the Great (c. 400–461), and yet others identify Saint Isidore of Seville (c. 560–636) as the writer. The fact that such great saints (all of whom are Doctors of the Church) are nominated as possible authors reflects the very high esteem in which the work was held.

But there are various good reasons for doubting the historical accuracy of each of the above-mentioned attributions. Firstly, the style of the Latin is that of the middle or late medieval period rather than the more classical style of Saints Ambrose, Leo the Great, or Isidore of Seville. Moreover, there are numerous passages where the author seems to be making direct reference to principles and phrases from the Rule of Saint Benedict, which would not be expected with any of the three saints proposed.

There is, however, another and much more probable saint to whom the authorship of the work has been attributed:

Saint Leo IX, who served as pope during the turbulent years of the eleventh century. He had a background in, and close affinity to, Benedictine monasticism, and Saint Benedict was a special patron of his. Although relatively little known to most Catholics today, Leo IX was one of the greatest and most revered popes of the Middle Ages. The short biography of him, included in this volume, reveals that his life was distinguished both by humble sanctity, diligence in his pastoral duties, and astonishing miracles.

The attribution of the work to Leo IX is supported by no less an authority than Saint Peter Canisius (1521–97), who is himself a Doctor of the Church. He gives three reasons for crediting Saint Leo IX as the author:

1. The oldest existing manuscripts, which date from the eleventh or twelfth centuries, give the author as "Leo" or "Pope Leo," but none include the designation "Leo the Great."

2. There are numerous clear references to the Rule of Saint Benedict, which seems to rule out Ambrose, Leo the Great, or Isidore as possible authors, but which match perfectly with the well-known devotion of Leo IX to that great monastic saint.

3. The style of the Latin very closely resembles that of the other writings of Saint Leo IX and

the form of expression typical of the era in which he lived.

It is pertinent to make some comment in these introductory notes on the nature of the vices and virtues. The literal meanings of the terms "vice" (*vitium*) and "virtue" (*virtus*) are "weakness" and "strength," respectively. The vices are not in themselves sins; rather, they are propensities or tendencies to sin. Thus, for example, impatience or irritability are both vices, for they may readily lead a person into sinful words or actions. But simply to experience these as feelings is not a sin, unless it leads to some voluntary action or expression, or conscious consent of the will.

However, it is to be noted that in certain cases, a thought (if it is deliberately cultivated and entertained) can also constitute an action. An example of this would be the case of lust, or sexual attraction of an illicit nature. Such tendencies of illicit sexual attraction are not in themselves necessarily sinful, since they do not always arise from a person's free will and are of purely natural origin. But if illicit sexual attractions are deliberately cultivated (even if accompanied by no actions), they easily become sinful.

It is also to be noted that persons whose actions are sinful may actually possess many virtues. For example, it is possible that a sinful person may possess self-discipline, prudent restraint of speech, and patience. Such virtues may, indeed, even occasionally be misdirected towards sinful goals. Furthermore, a particular trait can cease to be a virtue and become a vice if unmoderated or taken to extremes. For example, generosity, if excessive and ungoverned by wisdom, could become improvidence and prodigality. Love of justice, if inflexible and untampered by mercy, can easily become severity or harshness.

For the person who aspires to live a life of goodness and uprightness, the cultivation of the virtues and the active fighting against the vices is essential. The more a person is aware of the presence of specific vices in his character, the better equipped he will be to resist their influence and temptations. Moral goodness, which the virtues help to achieve, not only leads to the heavenly rewards which Christ has promised us but also is conducive to happiness and peace in this present life. Conversely, sin (if unrepented and unatoned) leads not only to the eternal misery of hell but also generally tends to make a person unhappy and unsuccessful in the present life as well.

In the dialogue which follows, a particular virtue is identified as a remedy for each vice. These virtues allow the propensity or impulse to sin to be checked and controlled by offering an opposing thought or consideration which cancels and rebukes each temptation. The translational approach adopted here aims at creating a convincing sense of a dialogue (including many instances of irony and colloquial language), with the vices and virtues each appearing as characters which address the soul. Descriptions of these various characters, which are intended to be personifications of each respective vice or virtue, have been added by the translator for the purpose of lending color to interlocutors in each dialogue. The scriptural verses quoted in the work are translations from the Vulgate text used by Leo, reflecting the sense in which he himself cites them.

From the popular circulation of the work in the Middle Ages, it is clear that many readers from that period found the dialogue extremely useful and edifying. It is the sincere hope of the present translator that many contemporary readers will also find this beloved and classic work similarly instructive and enjoyable, and that Saint Leo IX will prove to be an effective and wise spiritual director for today's Catholics.

And may Jesus Christ, who is Himself the "Virtue of God,"[1] assist each of us following the path of goodness and wisdom which leads to the eternal joys of heaven.

Sancte Leo, ora pro nobis!
Fr. Robert Nixon, OSB
Abbey of the Most Holy Trinity,
New Norcia, Western Australia

---

[1] 1 Corinthians 1:24.

THE LIFE OF POPE SAINT LEO IX

POPE SAINT LEO IX, whose baptismal name was Bruno, was born in the year of Our Lord 1002 in Alsace, a fertile, verdant, and richly wooded region of France, extending from the border of Switzerland to the border of Germany. He was the only son of a certain Hugh, a distinguished and honorable man of the highest wealth and most exalted nobility, being count of the French regions of Nordgau, Eguisheim, and Dabo, as well as a cousin to the Holy Roman emperor, Conrad II. Even as a child, Bruno distinguished himself for his angelic sanctity and precocious intelligence. At the age of five, he was entrusted to the care of Berthold, the bishop of the French diocese of Toul, from whom he received a comprehensive instruction in both classical learning and sacred doctrine. Bruno soon gained the admiration and esteem of all who knew him on account of his prodigious memory and the acuity of his understanding, as well as his unfailing humility and charity.

It was during his childhood years that Bruno chose Saint Benedict as a particular patron and beloved guide for himself. This resulted from a remarkable and curious miracle in which the life of young Bruno was spared through the intervention of this great saint. Once, while Bruno was enjoying a well-earned vacation from his studies at one of his parents' rural castles, it happened that a venomous toad stealthily crept into the bed chamber of the boy and concealed itself there in a dark corner. That night, as Bruno slept, the toad leapt upon him. At this, the boy woke up suddenly in a panic to find this loathsome creature resting on his person. The toad then bit the young lad on the throat, letting its vile poison flow into the gaping wound. Upon hearing the fear-stricken cries of Bruno, the entire household rushed to his bedchamber to see what was amiss. There, they found the boy in pain with a festering and inflamed wound upon his neck. He described to them the monstrous toad which had attacked him, but no trace of the hellish amphibian could be found.

The most expert physicians were summoned to treat Bruno, but without success. Indeed, for the next two months, the hapless youth became steadily worse, and his family began to despair of his chances of recovery.

But although these natural and human remedies proved ineffective, divine healing was given to Bruno. For one night, he beheld a vision of a man of venerable appearance robed in a monastic habit and surrounded by streams of refulgent light. He appeared to be descending from heaven through the skies, until he entered young Bruno's room through the window. In one hand, he held a crucifix, which he touched gently to the boy's forehead. And instantly, he was restored to perfect health!

Bruno had no doubt that the man whom he had seen in his vision and who had healed his illness was none other than Saint Benedict, the patriarch of all monks of the West. And from that time, Bruno had a deep devotion to Benedict and recited the office of the saint every day for the remainder of his life. And he did everything he possibly could, as a bishop and then as pope, to support Benedictine monasteries.

In due course, Bruno was ordained to the priesthood. His ministry was characterized by diligence and devotion, which was well supported by his prudence, wisdom, and erudition. Soon, he was consecrated as bishop of the important diocese of Toul, which he governed effectively and fruitfully for over two decades.

At this point in history, the governance of the Church in Rome was highly unstable and tainted by corruption. Moreover, there was a lack of certainty in many circles about whether it was the Holy Roman emperor or the college of cardinals in Rome who had the right to select a pope. Because of this confusion, there were frequently two rival claimants to the papal crown; indeed, at one point in the eleventh century, no less than three bishops each asserted themselves to be the legitimate pope. Pope Damasus II, Leo's predecessor, had died in 1048, and the Holy Roman emperor, in conference with an assembly of German bishops and some cardinals, chose Bruno to be the next pope.

In humble (though misguided) obedience, Bruno accepted this imperial decision. Accordingly, he set out to Rome, attired in his new papal regalia, to assume his new role. On the way, he met two monks. One was Saint Hugh, of the great abbey of Cluny, and the other was a young monk named Hildebrand, who would eventually become Pope Saint Gregory VII. They both expressed dismay that Bruno had accepted his appointment as pope and explained that it was not up to the Holy Roman emperor to choose the pontiff. Bruno, seeing the wisdom of their counsel, immediately removed his papal regalia and continued to Rome in the humble attire of a pilgrim. Yet, once he had arrived, all the clergy and cardinals of Rome (acting upon the advice of Hildebrand) enthusiastically and unanimously elected him as their new supreme pontiff. And thus Bruno ascended the Petrine throne (supported by both the college of cardinals and the Holy Roman emperor), taking for himself the name of Leo IX.

As pope, Leo was extremely effective. He fought strenuously against corruption within the Church (which was then widespread) and worked to strengthen education and discipline among the clergy and to enforce priestly celibacy.

He continued to be distinguished by his noble sanctity and sincere piety. A veritable multitude of astonishing miracles occurred during his life, one of which will be recounted here.

During Leo's pontificate, the king of Denmark possessed, amongst his many treasures and curiosities, a particularly splendid parrot. This noble and sagacious bird not only was blessed with glorious, polychromatic plumage but also had the ability to speak with a voice that seemed to be human. Now, when the king heard reports of the great sanctity and wisdom of Pope Leo IX, he resolved to send this fine bird to the holy pontiff as a gift. Amazingly, as the bird was being transported, it spontaneously began to say:

> All ye who hear me, know
> That to the pope I go;
> I'm off to my new home
> In great and noble Rome!"[2]

And the parrot continued to repeat these verses as it travelled along its route to Rome.

After it was presented to Leo, a very close rapport at once sprang up between the pontiff and his new feathered

---

[2] These lines (and those which follow) have been freely adapted from the original Latin text in order to produce rhyming verses.

companion. When the bird was first taken into his presence, it is said to have uttered the following verses:

> O Leo, gracious pope,
> In whom Christ's Church does hope,
> Most blest am I to meet thee,
> Rejoicing, do I greet thee!

Furthermore, it is reported that Leo, whenever fatigued or anxious with the demands of his pontifical office, would frequently derive great consolation and diversion from his conversations and verbal exchanges with this most talented bird.

This miracle, though apparently trivial in itself, attests to the fact that the working of divine power to achieve wondrous results was a conspicuous and regular part of Saint Leo's life. Another miracle, which happened towards the end of his life, reveals the extent of his compassion to those who are afflicted by suffering and his mystical closeness to Christ Himself.

It was the habit of Leo to go out at night incognito and wander the streets of Rome, accompanied by a single servant. During these nocturnal excursions, he would give alms and assistance to any beggars or needy pilgrims he encountered. It happened that on one night, he came across a particularly wretched beggar huddled in a corner. This beggar was not only afflicted by the most dire and squalid poverty but also infected with the dreaded disease of leprosy. The heart of

Leo was at once touched with the deepest compassion for this suffering man. Without hesitation, he took him back to the pontifical palace. There, he gave him his very own bed to sleep on and replaced the filthy rags he had been wearing by some of his own finest garments. Meanwhile, Leo himself took his rest on a spare couch.

Early the next morning, the saint went in to see how the leprous beggar had slept. But, to his great surprise, no trace of him could be found! Although the doors of the bedchamber had been locked, the mysterious beggar had vanished entirely.

The following night, Leo had a dream in which Christ appeared to him. He was noble and radiant in form but clothed in the exact same garments which Leo had given to the beggar.[3] And thus it was revealed to the holy pontiff that it was Christ Himself to whom He had shown compassion and care in the person of the wretched leper.

Leo's successor, Pope Victor III, described his predecessor as "a new and glorious light to the world who renewed and restored God's Holy Church." He also recounts that it was Leo's custom to make a devotional procession from the Lateran Basilica to Saint Peter's Basilica in the solitary hours of the night, with bare feet and clad in a penitential habit, chanting the psalms and praying fervently for the

---

[3] An almost identical incident is related in the life of Saint Martin of Tours.

Church. It was the practice of the holy pope to perform this secret act of piety and penance three times every week.

Saint Leo IX died in the year of Our Lord 1054, by which stage he was already popularly venerated as a living saint. Contemporary sources testify to the vast multitude of miraculous healings which occurred at his tomb following his burial. As well as writing numerous letters and decrees, Leo IX wrote *The Battle of the Virtues and Vices*—a remarkable and timeless literary masterpiece which amply displays both his profound wisdom into the Christian spiritual life and his penetrating and subtle insights into human psychology.

Author's Introduction

The apostolic voice of Saint Paul cries out throughout the entire world addressing zealously and boldly the attentive ears and hearts of all the faithful. It gives to them a timely and dire warning, lest they should grow complacent in their apparent state of security. For in resonant tones, it proclaims, "Whosoever wishes to live devoutly in Christ Jesus is destined to suffer persecutions."[4]

And this was indeed the truth for the faithful during those early years of the new-born Church, when Saint Paul penned those fateful words. For in those dark and dire days, everyone who adhered to Christian faith faced daily the perils of persecution, exiles, torture, and martyrdom.

But today, for those who wish to live devoutly in the faith of Jesus Christ, there are no longer the dangers of chains, or beatings, or whippings, or prisons, or cruel devices of torture, or crosses—at least, not in any literal sense. Such things have long passed into history for most Christians. How, therefore, can the words of Saint Paul continue to

---

[4] 2 Timothy 3:12.

ring true when he says that all who wish to live devoutly in Christ Jesus will suffer persecutions? Is it perhaps that there are, in our own times, no one who truly wishes to live devoutly, and that it is for this reason that the tortures and perils of the earlier times now exist no more? Such a foolish proposal is very clearly and manifestly untrue, for amongst the multitude of Christians, there are certainly still a great number who fervently wish to live devoutly.

Rather, the sentence of Saint Paul must be understood in a broad and metaphoric manner, taking the word "persecution" in its most general sense. For there are indeed many within the bosom of Holy Mother Church who *do* sincerely desire to live piously and devoutly in the faith of Jesus Christ, and who endure slander, condemnation, insults, derision, and mockery. But even this cannot be the same as the "persecution" of which Saint Paul speaks, and which he says that *all* who wish to live devoutly will suffer. For there are a great many other devout people who never suffer from slanders, condemnation, insults from others— or anything of that kind.

Hence, we may conclude that the apostle's words are to be understood in a different and even more subtle manner. For they must refer to some form of persecution or a conflict which is a universal experience for all who aspire to follow Christ.

But what could this persecution and conflict be? I suggest that it is nothing other than the battle between the vices and the virtues, which takes place within the heart of each and every human being, every single day of our lives. The enemies in this battle—the vices and temptations which infect our fallen nature—are invisible and internal. But, as experience teaches us, they are constant and unrelenting in their assaults. For pride always arises to attack and persecute humility; vainglory assaults fear of the Lord; counterfeit piety tries to undermine true holiness; and rebellion tries to overthrow obedience.

We see a veritable multitude of such conflicts arise, entailing each of the following oppositions:

- envy against fraternal charity
- hatred against love
- detraction against just correction
- wrath against patience
- severity against gentleness
- self-satisfaction against respect for others' feelings
- worldly melancholy against spiritual joy
- sloth against energetic virtue
- dissolute wandering against firm stability
- despair against faithful hope
- avarice against detachment from the world
- stinginess against generosity

- thievery and fraud against innocence
- concealment and deception against truthfulness
- gluttony against moderation
- inane elation against holy sorrow
- garrulity against prudent restraint
- fleshly desire and lust against purity and chastity
- spiritual fornications against purity of heart
- worldly attachment against longing for our heavenly homeland

All of these oppositions arise within us and wage their tumultuous wars upon the battlefields of our hearts. What is this, then, if not to suffer persecutions? For the one who wishes to live piously and devoutly finds himself persecuted by a multitude of vices, each seeking to overthrow the virtues and to lead the soul away from God.

O how hard and how bitter are the forces of pride, and all its malign companions and heinous henchmen! For these diabolic vices cast the very angels from the heavens and caused the first human beings to be expelled from the garden of paradise. This dark army of wickedness, whose commander is pride and whose soldiers are all the other vices, never ceases to persecute and pursue the soul which aspires to the kingdom of heaven. But in response, we may assemble our own army, composed of the virtues of Christ, ready to enter into battle and to defend ourselves against every temptation and every attack of the foe.

In the dialogue which follows, the vices will each seek to deceive and corrupt the human soul. But the virtues, in turn, will respond, putting up powerful and effective defenses.

O Reader, let us venture forth and see how this conflict—this epic battle for mastery of the soul—will transpire.

PRIDE IS PUT TO FLIGHT
BY HUMILITY

THE FIRST OF THE vices, Pride, arrives on the scene. He is clad in a brightly colored military uniform covered with golden medals and adorned with shiny epaulettes. A fiery gleam burns in his eyes, and an arrogant, disdainful smile (or rather, grimace) rests on his self-satisfied mouth. With a supercilious and haughty air, he says to the soul:

Listen to me, O Soul! Give heed to my words, for I will speak to you frankly.

You and I both know that you are undoubtedly better than almost everyone else, in respect to your words, your knowledge, your wealth, and your honors. In fact, you easily surpass most other people in virtually all talents and all gifts of the body, mind, and spirit! Why deny it? So you *should* look down on these others and honestly recognize yourself to be better since (if you look into your heart) you *know* that you actually are better than they!

Humility arrives in time to hear the speech of Pride. Humility wears a simple but clean and well-cut suit and carries himself with gentleness and quietness. Raising his wise and penetrating eyes with quiet and unostentatious authority, he responds thus:

O Soul, do not listen to the voice of Pride! For he seeks to deceive you—to puff you up only so that he may laugh when you fall down. He pretends to be your greatest supporter and most loyal advocate, but really he is the sworn enemy of your happiness and salvation.

Instead of hearing the voice of Pride, it behooves you to "remember that thou are but dust and ashes,"[5] as Scripture puts it. And "you are fashioned by the earth, and no more than a worm."[6] Whatever you might be, however great you might be, ask yourself this question: "Am I greater than the one who was the most exalted of all the angels?" Indeed, was there anyone who was more splendid and magnificent than the angel known as Lucifer, the Prince of Light? But he, through his wicked pride, was cast down to the darkest depth of hell! Now will you, who are a mere mortal, dare to exalt yourself, just as he did? Do you wish to share his sin and so share his utterly wretched fate?

Remember that as long as you live this earthly life, your condition is one of extreme fragility and weakness. You

---

[5] Genesis 3:19.
[6] Job 25:6.

are burdened with more limitations than you know, as a wise man once wrote: "The mortal body weighs down the soul, and our earthly dwelling place constrains the spirit which aspires to many things."[7] How lethal and heavy is the darkness of pride! How easily can it drag down the soul of us human beings, who inhabit bodies fashioned from the earth! For it caused the fall even of that formerly radiant and mighty being, the angel once known as the "Morning Star" and the "Bearer of Light," whom we still call "Lucifer."[8]

Listen, therefore, to the words of the One who is Himself the immortal light and the source of all light, the One who is Truth itself. He tells us, "Whoever follows me shall not walk in darkness, but will have the light of life."[9] And on another occasion, He gave us this most prudent admonition: "Learn from me, for I am meek and humble of heart; and you shall find rest for your souls."[10]

Hear, O vain Pride, the voice of Christ, the Master of humility: "All who exalt themselves shall be humbled, but everyone who humbles themselves will be exalted."[11]

---

[7] Wisdom 9:15.

[8] *Lucifer* means "bearer of light" and was an appellation given to the morning star.

[9] John 8:12.

[10] Matthew 11:29.

[11] Luke 14:11.

And in the writings of the prophets, do we not read: "Upon whom will my Spirit rest, apart from the one who is humble and quiet, and who fears my words?"[12] Listen also to what the apostle Saint Paul said, speaking of Our Lord Jesus Christ, our God and Savior:

> He was in the form of God,
> Yet He did not cling to equality with God,
> But emptied Himself, accepting the form of a
>   servant.
> And having accepted our human condition,
> He became humbler yet,
> Even to accepting death, death on a cross.[13]

If the One who possessed all the fullness of Divine Majesty was prepared to humble Himself in this radical way, then surely it does not behoove us mere mortals, who are but weak and fragile creatures, to extoll ourselves with foolish pride! Take care, O Soul, and do not let this malicious fiend, Pride, who is the captain of all the vices, gain possession of you.

---

[12] Isaiah 66:2.
[13] Philippians 2:6–11.

VAINGLORY IS REBUKED
BY FEAR OF THE LORD

NEXT, VAINGLORY APPEARS and approaches the soul. This vice is clad in a brilliant white robe and wearing rings on his fingers, displaying what appear to be precious gems. But a closer inspection reveals that the apparently brilliant robe is, in fact, made of filthy and stained cloth, and merely clumsily painted over with white, and the jewels, which looked like precious gems, are pieces of counterfeit. Vainglory holds a mirror in one hand, is constantly anxiously checking and adjusting his appearance. This vice says to the soul:

Achieve whatever praiseworthy things are possible for you, and do all the good and notable things you can! Then make sure that you show these good deeds to other people so that you will be described as good and declared to be holy by all, and recognized as one of those specially chosen by God. That way, no one will ever dare to look down upon you or despise you. Rather, everyone will show you the respect you truly deserve!

Let them see your good works, and they will give praise to God! And, more importantly, they will also give praise to *you*.

Meanwhile, Fear of the Lord has been sitting nearby, reading from a small volume of Sacred Scripture. Upon hearing the voice of Vainglory, he stands up to his full height. He is dressed in black and has an intelligent and serious expression on his face. Fear of the Lord then says to the soul:

This is foolish and fatuous advice, so typical of the voice of Vainglory!

My friend, if you do any good works, don't do them for the sake of rewards which are only transitory and illusory but rather for those honors which will last forever. Don't make a display of your merits, but keep them hidden away from human view as much as you are able. And if you are not able to do this always (as is almost inevitably the case), at least *try* to do so and sincerely desire to do so. Above all, shun the arrogance of parading your supposed merits before others! For such arrogance almost always comes before a fall.

Of course, though, you are not guilty of any sin if other people *do* sometimes recognize your good works and praise you for it—as long as gaining this praise was never your principal motivation. Hence it is that we find that our Redeemer spoke two sentences, which are apparently in contradiction, but not so in reality. For at one point, Christ said, "When you give alms, let your left hand not know what your right hand is doing. But let your almsgiving be in secret, so that your Father who sees all that is done in secret shall reward you."[14] But a little earlier, He had exhorted us, "Let them see your good works, so that they may glorify your Father who is in heaven."[15]

The key is to be constantly cautious, lest what Our Lord declared concerning the hypocrites may ever be applied to *you* as well. For He said of such hypocrites, "They do all their good works just so that they will be praised by others."[16] And, reproving such people, He asserted, "I tell you solemnly, they have already received their rewards!"[17]

O Soul, examine yourself and your true motives *very* carefully in all the things which you do! Take care that you never become infected with the hidden taint of pride, or that vainglory does not become your secret and ulterior motive. Otherwise, you might end up like those who glory in empty signs and displays, but come, on the Day of Judgment, to hear the dreaded words of everlasting damnation: "Behold, I saw the morning star fall from the sky like lightning!"[18]

---

[14] Matthew 6:3–4.
[15] Matthew 5:16.
[16] Matthew 23:5.
[17] Luke 18:11.
[18] Luke 10:18.

3

COUNTERFEIT PIETY IS
EXPOSED BY TRUE HOLINESS

COUNTERFEIT PIETY THEN walks in. He has his hands clasped in apparently devout prayer, and has multiple sets of rosary beads hanging from his belt which jangle noisily. Despite his evident attempts to maintain a pious demeanor, his eyes constantly move about shiftily, as if he is keen to see whether or not anyone is looking at him. He speaks thus to the soul:

My friend, you know that you have no genuine good inclinations within you and that if people saw you as you really are, they would inevitably condemn you for not meeting their standards and expectations. For everyone is ready to judge you the moment they have the chance!

So, here's what you should do: study carefully what other people expect and admire, and then deliberately cultivate for yourself a false exterior which meets these expectations. If necessary, project to the world an image of someone who is quite different from the innermost desires of your heart.

Never let your real self and your true feelings and nature be seen by anyone! In this way, all will come to call you good and holy and treat you with reverence and respect.

But True Holiness appears. She looks just like any regular person, and you would not spot her for who she is immediately. Yet an aura of kindness, honesty, and reverence emanates from her. She answers the temptation of Counterfeit Piety—who, in fact, is a distant cousin of hers—with the following words:

My friend, don't listen to this wicked and foolish advice of my misguided kinsman, Counterfeit Piety! If you recognize your own sinfulness and wicked tendencies, that is indeed a fine and beneficial thing. But if this is the case, do not just try to *appear* to be something else than what you are, but instead try to *become* something else! Why be content with *seeming* to be good when you could be good in reality? Can a false appearance ever be preferable to the real thing?

Don't forget those words frighteningly spoken by Our Lord Jesus when He said, "Woe to you, scribes and Pharisees! Hypocrites! You are like cups which are clean and polished on the outside, but inside are filled with filth."[19] And a little later, He continued, "You are like whitewashed tombs, which seem beautiful on the outside, but inside are

---

[19] Matthew 23:25.

filled with the bones of the dead and with all kinds of foulness."[20] And did He not condemn those who are wolves on the inside but conceal their true natures beneath the clothing of sheep? And what are any external pretensions to goodness apart from such deceptive garments of disguise?

My friend, since you already aspire to be regarded as holy, it must be plain to you already that holiness is an intrinsically good and desirable thing. So why settle for false holiness when you could very readily cultivate true holiness? Why be content with appearances when the reality is so generously offered to you?

To seek to appear to be something which you are not is both wearying and fruitless. But to seek to become truly holy and good is to become the person who God created you to be! Do this, and you shall find perfect happiness.

---

[20] Matthew 23:27.

4

REBELLION IS SUBDUED
BY HOLY OBEDIENCE

REBELLION THEN ARRIVES. He strides in noisily, knocking things about as he passes by and muttering curses under his breath. At his side is a sheath containing a sharp sword, and he holds a shield on one arm bearing his coat of arms—a braying, prancing donkey, with the motto inscribed underneath "Non serviam" (I shall not serve). He has a proud look in his eyes and speaks arrogantly:

O Soul, why should you be bound to follow the whims of people who are no better than yourself? Were you created to be a slave of the system, to obey people blindly, even when they know less than you?

Really, it should be *you*, not them, who is giving the orders! For who is there among them who equals you in all your intelligence or hard work? As long as you obey the commands of the Lord, you need not bother about obeying anybody else. Did Our Lord Himself not say, "Call no one on earth your master"?[21]

To this, Holy Obedience, who is wearing a monastic habit and exudes peace and tranquility, responds:

O Soul, if you really and sincerely want to obey the commands of God, you must learn to submit yourself also to the legitimate commands of other human beings. Our Lord Himself clearly articulated this principle when He said, "Whoever hears you, hears Me; and whoever refuses to hear you, refuses to hear Me."[22]

I know what you will say! "That is all well and good, as long as the person who is giving the command is acting as the agent of God. But what if he is not?" To this, I would respond that *all* legitimate authority comes from God. For, as the apostle Saint Paul wrote, "There is no power or authority except that given by God. All powers that exist, exist only by the ordination and disposition of God. And so whoever resists any legitimate human authority, resists God!"[23]

It is not up to subordinates to pass judgment on their superiors. For Our Lord Himself has given instructions about how superiors ought to conduct themselves, and no one else need add to these. For instance, He said, addressing

---

[21] Matthew 23:8–10.
[22] Luke 10:16.
[23] Romans 13:1.

the future shepherds of the Church, "You know that the rulers of the pagans lord it over them, and those who yield power are called 'philanthropists.' But with you, it must not be so!"[24] And in the same vein, He declared, "If any of you wishes to be great, he should make himself the servant of all."[25] And, offering Himself as a perfect example and model of this paradigm of leadership, He said, "The Son of Man came not to be served, but to serve."[26]

These instructions and admonitions are all directed at those who exercise leadership and authority. But how well these precepts are fulfilled is a matter for the Lord to decide, not for subordinates to judge!

Accordingly, Christ also gave firm directions to those who find themselves in subordinate states, exhorting them to obedience to properly constituted authorities. For, speaking of the scribes and Pharisees, He said to His disciples, "They sit upon the chair of Moses. Therefore do what they say! But do not do what they do."[27]

Accordingly, the duty of the subordinate is to obey, not to judge. For rest assured that there is One who *will* judge, and it is this One that everyone, both those who command and those who obey, shall answer to in the end.

---

[24] Luke 22:25–26.
[25] Mark 10:43.
[26] Matthew 20:28.
[27] Matthew 23:2.

5

ENVY IS REBUKED BY
FRATERNAL CHARITY

Next, Envy arrives on the scene. Her most striking character-istic is piercing, bright green eyes. These dart about constantly to see if anyone seems to be more highly favored or fortunate then her. Her expression is bitter and resentful as she speaks thus to the soul:

Look at those people, the ones who have been placed in charge of things; they're so satisfied with themselves! They've been given everything they could want—power, position, prosperity—on a silver platter.

But how are they any better or less deserving than *you* are? Why should you not be treated as equal to them? In fact, why should you not be their superior? You could defi-nitely do a much better job than they are doing! You could achieve so much more!

These others—they should not be your superiors at all, nor even your equals!

But Fraternal Charity is present as well. He looks upon the world, and other people, with a good-natured smile. Upon hearing Envy's words, he is quick to offer the soul some better advice:

Do not listen to these thoughts of Envy, for they will only poison your heart with bitterness and take away the peace and happiness which could easily be yours!

Reflect for a moment on how much safer and more secure it is to occupy a lower place then a higher one. For those who are placed in an exalted rank immediately find themselves a prey to all kind of stress and pressure. They face risk and trials, and the eyes of everyone are on them, always ready to judge and find faults in everything they do! Would you really want this, and all the extra burdens and responsibilities, for yourself? For the higher you climb, the harder it is to maintain your position, the more enemies, rivals, and critics you will have, and the worse will be your fall, if it comes!

And when you look at others and envy their high status, are you not doing exactly the same thing that Satan did when he envied God Himself? And it was the envy of the devil which brought about his own ruin, and which brought death and sorrow into this world. My friend, reflect upon the words of Scripture: "It was through the devil's envy that death entered the world. And all those who imitate him will come to belong to him!"[28]

The kind of thoughts and feelings which Envy would sow in your heart cannot help in the least. If you really want to get ahead, work hard on yourself, but do not direct ill-feeling at others. You won't hurt them, but will only make yourself bitter and destroy your own happiness!

---

[28] Wisdom 2:24.

6

Hatred Is Quelled by Love

The next two characters who arrive one the scene are the vice of Hatred and the virtue of Love. Both of these have the form of clouds. That cloud of Hatred is black and turbulent. Alternately, gusts of chilling cold and searing heat gush forth from it. Love, on the other hand, is a rose-colored cloud, with a steady glow of radiant light coming from deep within it. This light illuminates its surroundings and suffuses everything upon which it falls with an iridescent shimmer, imparting a remarkable beauty to all to which it comes close.

The black cloud of Hatred speaks first in a tone of menacing thunder. It says:

O Soul, it is absurd for you to love the person who opposed you in all things! It is ridiculous to say that you love those who berate and insult you, who unjustly thwart your efforts, who accuse you falsely, and who arrogantly put themselves ahead of you in all that they say and do. Would they treat you like this if they cared anything at all for you?

Indeed, unless they had complete contempt for you, they would not act in this way towards you! And are *you* now expected to love them? Don't even think about it!

But a gentle and harmonious voice then emanates from the radiant and roseate cloud of Love. It refutes the suggestions of Hatred in the following terms:

O Soul, it is true that, on a purely human level, the things you describe are hard to love, and I cannot pretend that even I, who am Love itself, like to experience them! Nevertheless, does that mean that I should cease to love the true image of God, which each and every human being bears? Christ Himself, as He underwent the torments of the cross, did not cease to love his enemies, who tortured and killed him. And even before this, He had given us a commandment: "Love your enemies, and do good to those who hate you. Pray for those who insult and calumniate you, and then you shall be truly sons or daughters of your Father who is in heaven."[29]

And the wise king Solomon, who is later quoted by Paul, advises us, "If your enemy is hungry, supply him with food, and if he is thirsty, then give him something to drink. In this way, you shall pour hot coals upon his head!"[30] And the apostle Paul also exhorts us, "Do not be conquered by

---

[29] Luke 6:27.
[30] Proverbs 25:12–13; Romans 12:20.

evil, but rather overcome evil by doing good."[31] The apostle Saint John likewise issues a dire warning against those who nurture hate within their hearts, speaking thus, "Whoever hates his brother is a murderer! And you know that no murderer can have within himself eternal life."[32] And in another place, he writes, "Whoever hates his brother walks in the darkness, and abides in the darkness; and such a person does not know where he is going, for the darkness has rendered his eyes blind and unseeing."[33] What a pernicious and perilous poison is hate! And its only effective antidote is its opposite and antithesis, love.

But you may object, saying, "Surely, it suffices if I love those who love me!" Note that Our Lord Himself explicitly contradicts this point of view. For He says, "If you love those who love you, what reward can you expect? For even the tax-collectors do as much!"[34] These words are *very* clear and there is no room for error or misinterpretation—we must love *all* of our brothers and sisters, not only those who love us. Why? Because Christ has commanded us thus! And it is not to be doubted that "whoever hates his brother remains in death; but whoever loves them abides in God, and God abides in him."[35]

---

[31] Romans 12:21.

[32] 1 John 3:15.

[33] 1 John 2:11.

[34] Matthew 5:46.

[35] 1 John 3:13.

O Soul, strive to vomit forth the foul and bitter gall of hatred and animosity which now ferments within you! Instead, drink deeply of the sweet nectar of charity, of love for all human beings—or rather, love of the image of God which exists in each and every human soul. Nothing is more sweet and delightful than love, nothing is more truly blessed than charity. For "God is love,"[36] as Saint John declared. And the illustrious preacher to the nations, Saint Paul, said that "the love of God is suffused into our hearts, through the Holy Spirit which is given unto us."[37]

Hence it is that love is said to cover up a multitude of sins. And, accordingly, it is wisely and veraciously written: "Charity can cover up any offence."[38]

---

[36] 1 John 4:8; 16.
[37] Romans 5:5.
[38] 1 Peter 4:8.

7

DETRACTION IS REFUTED BY JUST CORRECTION

DETRACTION THEN ARRIVES. He is mumbling bitterly to himself in an undertone, with a sullen expression on his face. After kicking the ground angrily a few times, he says to the soul:

Alas! Who is able to tolerate the deplorable things which are going on around you? Who could turn a blind eye to all the incompetence, slackness, and wickedness which you see in your colleagues and confreres? For to do this, to ignore sin, is to give tacit consent to it!

At this point, Just Correction makes an appearance. His face and stature closely resembles that of Detraction, as if they are distant relatives. But whereas Detraction is surrounded by an aura of bitterness and uneasiness, Just Correction is perfectly calm and self-assured. He offers the following response to the words of his kinsman, Detraction:

O Soul, of course, one should never keep silence about crimes and works of evil, and one should never consent to, or ignore, such things when they happen. But it behooves us to correct our neighbors, when it is necessary, in a manner which is grounded in fraternal charity. We certainly shouldn't go about disparaging them behind their backs, as Detraction is accustomed to do!

But you might object to this, saying, "If I correct my brother or sister openly, they are likely to take offence at me. It won't do any good, and they won't end up listening at all to what I have to say. If I offer an open and frank correction, it won't bring about any good at all for anyone, but will only give rise to scandal and animosity!"

Well, to this observation, I say this: if correcting your neighbor openly is going to give rise to scandal and animosity, what do you think that detracting from his reputation and disparaging him behind his back is going to do? It will be much, much worse! The pages of Scripture testify to this, for it is written, "When you sit gossiping about your brother, you generate scandal against one who is the son of your mother!"[39]

Indeed, a person will typically feel more animosity and indignation when he finds out that you've been grumbling against him to others secretly than if you just offered your correction of feedback to him honestly and directly.

---

[39] Psalms 49:20.

And it is often the case that it is more prudent to remain silent about other people's faults rather than speaking out an inopportune time or in an inappropriate forum. The Lord Himself sometimes chooses to defer offering correction and reprimand to sinners, as is declared prophetically in the psalm: "You did these things, and yet I remained silent."[40]

But detractors and people given to private grumbling shouldn't image themselves to be practicing such wise prudence in hiding their true opinions and complaints from the people concerned. Hence it is that in the above quoted psalm, the very next line we read is: "Did you think that I am like you?"[41] This line shows that when God chooses to defer His correction or punishment of sinners, it is definitely not because He intends to grumble in secret about them. Heaven forbid such an impious thought! Rather, the Lord, in His infinite wisdom and mercy, waits for the most suitable time. This is because His corrections of sin are never intended as wrathful or destructive condemnations but rather as the seeds of repentance and renewal. The openness of the corrections which God offers the sinner are expressed in the following line of the same Psalm: "I shall correct you to your face."[42] In other words, God does

---

[40] Psalms 49:21.
[41] Psalms 49:21.
[42] Psalms 49:21.

not harbor secret resentment and indignation against those who offend Him or do wrong, as we are so apt to do.

But you might object further, claiming that it is not out of hatred but rather out of love that you grumble against your brother or sister. Really? I suggest that if you truly wished to act out of love, you would either correct them openly or not at all—but you certainly wouldn't instigate a campaign of disparagement and detraction against them!

For detraction, disparagement, and gossip are *never* acts of love. And they are never helpful or constructive. Ask yourself: Has any good ever come out of them? I think not! Thus it is that Saint Paul so perspicaciously counsels us: "Take care that you do not bite and devour one another; lest you end up consuming each other!"[43]

---

[43] Galatians 5:15.

8

WRATH IS CALMED BY PATIENCE

WITH A GREAT clamor and turbulence, Wrath then enters the scene. He is not in human form but has the likeness of an enormous and wild black horse. This horse has eyes which blaze piercingly like red-hot coals, and acrid smoke issues from its nostrils. Its hoofs stamp furiously on the ground, causing the earth to tremble.

But suddenly, it becomes still and turns its glowing red eyes steadily to the soul. It then speaks with a human voice, saying:

O Soul, the things which are being done against you simply *cannot* be tolerated! To put up with these things, making a great show of patience and equanimity, would be a sin! And if you meekly put up with these things now (even if that were possible), where it is going to lead? For surely, they will do worse things to you, and to others, in the future once they see that no one is going to take a stand against their misdeeds!

But Patience arrives. He bears in his hands reins and a bridle, which he deftly places upon Wrath, bringing him under his control. And in gentle but commanding tones, he responds to the temptations presented by Wrath, speaking thus to the soul:

Before acting on these hasty words, O Soul, I urge you to reflect a moment! If you call to mind the blessed passion of Our Lord and Savior, what do you witness, what example is provided for you? Did Christ not bear the most horrendous acts of injustice, wickedness, and cruelty against Himself, all with the utmost patience and equanimity? Saint Peter testifies to this when he writes, "Christ suffered for us, leaving us an example, so that we should follow His footsteps."[44]

And Jesus Himself told us that we should expect to suffer in this life, inviting us to emulate His own holy patience and endurance, when He said, "If they call the Master of the house Beelzebub, how much more will they ill-treat His servants?"[45] And in another place, He says similarly, "Since they have persecuted Me, they shall surely also persecute you."[46]

O Soul, ask yourself what is it that any of us suffer in comparison to what Our Lord suffered for us? For Jesus endured insult, mocking, contumelies, slaps, spittle, whips, the crown of thorns, and finally the atrocious horrors of the cross! And yet *we* get upset if someone says to us a single hurtful word and are thrown into dismay by one casual slight or disparagement. Why is it that we so often and

---

[44] 1 Peter 2:21.
[45] Matthew 10:25.
[46] John 15:20.

lightly forget that prophetic oracle: "Unless we suffer with Him, we shall not be crowned with Him"?[47]

It behooves us, therefore, to turn a deaf ear to the goading of wrath. Aptly does he appear in the form of a horse, rather than a human—for wrath is an irrational impulse born of pride. Whenever wrath flares up within us, we should call to mind the punishment which Our Lord tells us is its due. For He said, "Whoever is angry at his brother will be in danger of judgment, and whoever calls his brother a rebel shall be in danger before the council, and whoever calls his brother a fool shall be in danger of the fires of hell!"[48]

And immediately afterwards, Christ offers us an apt and effective remedy for these grave perils which result from wrath. "If you bring your offering to the altar, and recall there that your brother has something against you," He says, "then leave your offering before the altar and go and be reconciled to your brother first. Then, after you are reconciled, come back and make your offering."[49] In saying this, Christ is counseling us not to flee to the refuge of silent and contemplative prayer within the chamber of our heart until we have first done all that we reasonably can to be at peace with our brothers and sisters. For our offering

---

[47] 2 Timothy 2:5.
[48] Matthew 5:22.
[49] Matthew 5:23–24.

to God is indeed our prayer, and the altar on which it is offered is our own heart.

But the person who offers his prayer *without* making an effort to be reconciled and without striving to subdue the fires of rage within his heart, places his very soul at peril and risks the punishment which Jesus has previously described. And yet there are many who stubbornly refuse to forgive others and who (out of pride or self-righteousness) refuse to seek forgiveness from others for themselves! Alas, it is as if they have been somehow rendered completely oblivious to what the Son of God told us, and told us in very clear and emphatic terms: "If you do not forgive the sins of others, your heavenly Father will not forgive you your sins."[50]

But perhaps this does not suffice to convince you. For you may well say, "But they have done so very many things against me, and they do them so very often! Now, if it were once or twice, I would readily forgive and excuse them, but as it is, how can I possibly stop my anger from rising within me?" To this, I shall not respond but rather will let Our Lord Himself answer you. For on one occasion, Peter said to Him, "Lord, if my brother sins against me, how often should I forgive him? As many as seven times?" And to this, Christ replied, "Not seven times, I tell you, but seventy-seven times."[51]

---

[50] Matthew 6:15.
[51] Matthew 18:21–22.

How many people there are who foolishly and presumptuously take the punishment and vengeance of the misdeeds of others into their own hands instead of entrusting it to God! In doing this, not only do they interfere with the operations of divine justice (which would, in due course, have worked in their favor), but they even risk impairing punishment themselves. And alas for those who let wrath so dominate their hearts that they pour forth curses upon their brothers or sisters! For Scripture warns us that "cursers will not inherit the Kingdom of God."[52]

Ask yourself, O Soul, whatever it is that has stirred you to wrath, is it really worth such a high price? Is it more important to you than admission to the eternal joys of the kingdom of heaven? I hope that it is not.

---

[52] 1 Corinthians 6:10.

9

GENTLENESS DISARMS SEVERITY

NEXT, SEVERITY APPEARS on the scene. He is dressed in a very close-fitting suit and looks around with a disapproving frown. In his hand, he holds a rod, his favorite instrument of discipline, and seems impatient to put it to use. He says to the soul:

Listen to me, Soul, and think seriously. You are being altogether too mild, too lenient—a pushover! Do not these beasts, these fools, with whom you are compelled to interact daily, deserve a good thrashing more than mere gentle words? Their actions have merited harsh treatment, and it will teach them a good lesson they will not soon forget!

Gentleness is also present at this time. She is sitting down, with a sweet and kindly expression on her face. In response to Severity's exhortation, she then addresses the soul in soothing and dulcet tones:

O Soul, do not listen to this fallacious and harsh reasoning! Rather, call to mind the precepts of the apostle Saint Paul, and strive to follow them faithfully. For, speaking to his beloved disciple Timothy, he offers him the following sagacious counsel: "Do not correct a senior. Rather, I ask that you treat seniors as your fathers, and youths as your brothers, and older women as your mothers, and younger women as your sisters, displaying too all pure and chaste charity."[53]

This disposition of mildness is again articulated by Paul when he says, "A servant should not be contentious against his master but rather meek and gentle. We should be patient teachers, correcting those who go astray with modesty and charity."[54]

Truly, this vice of arrogant and judgmental severity is a greater and more pernicious evil when it flares up among subordinates than among superiors. And, indeed, it very often happens that when those in subordinate positions are corrected by their superiors, they are inflamed by resentment and defiance and immediately judge—and condemn—those whose role it is to lead them with unmitigated harshness and severity. Thus the good-willed correction offered to them by their caring superiors becomes for them an occasion of resentment and pride.

---

[53] 1 Timothy 5:2.
[54] 2 Timothy 2:24.

Alas, it is of precisely this type of situation that Scripture speaks when it warns us that "the one who corrects a mocker does himself an injury."[55]

On the other hand, when a person is able to accept a correction and constructive without bitterness and resentment, but even with equanimity and gratitude, it is a sure sign that wisdom and peace are flourishing in his heart. Thus is written: "If you correct a wise person, he will love you for it."[56]

O Soul, be gentle, even as Jesus was gentle; be meek as He was meek; and be patient, just as He was patient. For in doing this, you shall inherit not only the earth but the kingdom of heaven itself!

---

[55] Proverbs 9:7.
[56] Proverbs 9:8.

10

Self-Satisfaction Is Corrected and Reined In by Respect for Others' Feelings

Self-Satisfaction then enters. He has a smug grin and an abrasive manner, and he exudes self-assurance. This vice whispers to the soul, as if sharing some secret truth, saying:

You have God as your witness in heaven! He sees all that you do and knows all that you think and feel. He alone knows you truly, and He alone has the right to judge you. Why, then, should you care a jot what these other people think of you or say about you? What are they to you?

Ignore them! Dismiss them from your thoughts completely. For their opinions about you are their own business, but they should mean nothing to *you*!

The virtue Respect for Others' Feelings is also present. He also exudes confidence, but without any smugness or abrasiveness. Responding quietly, but with wisdom and firmness, he speaks thus:

In a sense, that is true. It *is* God alone who sees all and has the right to make absolute judgment on you and on any human soul. But that doesn't mean that you should disregard the feelings and thoughts of others completely! After all, they are your brothers and sisters, and charity demands that you give them your consideration.

If you can possibly avoid giving rise to occasions of grumbling or gossip, or reasons for scandal, you should certainly endeavor to do so. If you find that somehow a false rumor about you has gotten into circulation, you should make an effort to show the plain truth of the matter clearly. If it is completely ungrounded, you should simply deny it with all humility.

For scandal not only hurts those against whom it is directed but also imperils the morale and peace of all who come into contact with it. Thus it is that the apostle Saint Paul wisely warns us that we should take care that we give no occasion to the devil to gain any foothold through actions which may cause scandal to others (even if the actions in question are perfectly innocent in themselves).[57]

He said this in relation to the practice of eating food consecrated to idols. Indeed, he knew that such consecration did not matter at all, in an objective sense, since the idols were mere figments of people's imaginations and nothing in themselves. On the other hand, he realized that there

---

[57] See 1 Corinthians 8.

were other people to whom such a thing would cause scandal. So, out of respect for the feelings of others, he urges Christians to refrain from eating food consecrated to idols. In a like manner, we too should be sensitive to what others think and feel in all that we do—not in a servile way, or because we need their approval, but out of charity and respect for them.

11

WORLDLY MELANCHOLY IS PUT TO FLIGHT BY SPIRITUAL JOY

WORLDLY MELANCHOLY THEN arrives. She is dressed in black with black polish upon her fingernails, matching her raven-black hair, but contrasting dramatically with the deathly pallor of her skin. Her manner is languid and depressed. She speaks to the soul in tones of infinite weariness:

O Soul, what do you have to rejoice about since you see so very many unspeakably terrible things going on all around you? Look at the world you live in; look at what our society has become! There are so many causes for sorrow and heartbreak, which cannot be denied.

Also, think about all the people who are speaking and plotting against you and all the adversities which you continue to encounter and endure, all for the sake of your beliefs. Are these not a genuine and justified cause for the bitterest grief? Are they not a cause for an ocean of tears; shall they not summon forth from your poor heart innumerable sighs of desolation and melancholy? For this life is nothing but a badly-written tragedy, where every rose hides a thorn, and every ending is sad.

But Spiritual Joy soon follows. She appears to be related to Worldly Melancholy, for they are of similar appearance and stature. But Spiritual Joy, in contrast to the sable garments of Melancholy, wears a dress of bright blue. Her complexion has a healthy glow, and her hair is of the beautiful gold of the rising sun. Her face bears a radiant smile, and an aura of confident serenity surrounds her. Having listened patiently to the discourse of Worldly Melancholy, she responds thus to the soul:

My friend, through long experience, I know well that there are two possible causes for sorrow, or, rather, there are two types of sorrow, both quite distinct from each other. One form of sorrow is beneficial and healthy and leads the soul to penitence, reformation, and improvement. But the other form is pernicious and harmful, for it leads not to repentance or improvement but rather only to the dreadful dead end of despair! One form of sorrow, holy sorrow, leads to life, but the other only brings death.

Now, it is the second form of sorrow—Worldly Melancholy—which has just been speaking to you now and is trying to tempt you. For the reasons for being sad it offers should, if considered more properly, be causes of rejoicing to you rather than sorrow! It is true that there are many difficulties which you must undergo in this life, and many apparent tragedies and misfortunes take place, the reasons for which exceed our current understanding. No one can honestly deny this. But these should be a cause for awe and joyful expectation of what lies in the future, not of despair over the things of the present moment. For did not Christ, who is the Giver of all good gifts and the munificent Bestower of all joys, exhort us thus: "When people persecute you and speak all kind of calumny against you, then rejoice and be glad; for, behold, your reward shall be great in heaven!"[58]

Call to mind also the example of the apostles, which we find recounted in the book of Acts: "And the apostles left the council rejoicing, because they had been found worthy to suffer disgrace for the sake of the name of Jesus Christ."[59]

O Soul, don't let yourself be saddened by anything in this world, for it is all passing, and shall very soon vanish away like an insubstantial dream, a fleeting vision of the night. Set your heart, rather, on the things which are eternal, and direct your immortal soul to those realities which endure forever. Let your joy be grounded in the golden hope of heaven, and let your only real sadness be in the dread of losing that ineffable delight and glory!

---

[58] Matthew 5:11–12.
[59] Acts 5:41.

12

SLOTH IS REPROVED BY ENERGETIC VIRTUE

NEXT, SLOTH APPEARS on the scene. He walks slowly or, rather, shuffles along, dragging his feet lazily. His shoulders are slumped, and his eyes are dull and listless. Though his muscles appear to be weak and underdeveloped, a prominent paunch is visible beneath his ill-fitting clothes. In a sleepy voice, this vice speaks thus to the soul:

My friend, if you keep pushing yourself so hard, very soon you will wear yourself out completely! If you keep reading in the darkness of the night, your eyes will grow dim and blind. If you keep shedding tears of compunction in your prayers, you soon won't have any eyes left at all! And if you keep depriving yourself of much-needed sleep by rising diligently for vigils, you will end up driving yourself insane! And, on top of this, if you weigh yourself down with so many duties and tasks, when will you have leisure for contemplation and reflection?

Be like me, and take things easy! Look after yourself more, and don't push yourself. You are only flesh and blood, and you need your rest.

This listless and lethargic vice is quickly followed by its anti-dote and foe, Energetic Virtue. Energetic Virtue arrives with a springing step, walking with an almost march-like rhythm. Though his frame is no larger than that of Sloth, he appears to be much taller because his posture is notably erect and strong. Determination and energy are evident in the keen glint of his eyes and the strength of his jawline. In a resonant and author-itative tone, he speaks to the soul:

O Soul, do you imagine you are going to live forever in this world so that you can take your time about living your life and do just what pleases you, when and if you feel like it? Do you even know for sure if you will still be alive to-morrow? Or if you have just another hour to live?

No, indeed, you do not! *Carpe diem*, as the poet says. Seize the day! Your opportunities for good works, for penitence, and for prayer are all strictly limited. So you need to make the most of every single moment the good Lord grants you, for you have no idea of how many more you will be given. Constantly call to mind the dire warning of the Gospel: "Stay awake, for you know neither the day nor the hour."[60]

---

[60] Matthew 25:13.

Cast off the sloth and lassitude of the flesh; let the indefatigable energy of the heaven-bound spirit drive you forth! For the kingdom of heaven shall not be attained by the half-hearted and tepid, or the weak or the slothful. Rather, Christ tells us that it will be seized by violence[61]—in other words, by energy and determination! Your time on earth is short. Make each moment count towards achieving the eternal glory which is your destiny!

---

[61] Matthew 11:12.

13

DISSOLUTE WANDERING IS RESTRAINED BY FIRM STABILITY

DISSOLUTE WANDERING NEXT comes into the presence of the soul. This vice seems to be ambling around at random, constantly stopping and starting and changing direction purposelessly. It looks as if it is about to speak to the soul but then seems to think better of it and wanders off. After a little while though, it comes back again. This time, it addresses the soul in the following words:

If God is really everywhere and omnipresent, why keep yourself fixed in this one place? If you are not perfectly happy anywhere, or in any situation, the answer is simple: move on to somewhere else! God is just as close to you anywhere in the world, so come and go wherever and whenever you will.

The virtue opposed to Dissolute Wandering, Firm Stability, is also present. In fact, he has been there all along, sitting still upon a rock, assiduously perusing a hefty volume of sacred theology. He responds to the temptations of Dissolute Wandering, speaking thus:

If it is as you assert, that God is present everywhere (as indeed He is), then what possible benefit is there to you in moving from one place to another? If all physical locations are equally close to the omnipresent God, surely this place—where you are right now—is just as good as any other!

But perhaps you will object, saying, "If I look for something better than *this* (my current life, such as it is!), I shall surely find something better! For, as Our Lord said, the one who looks always finds." To this, I respond by asking you to call to mind Adam and Eve and how they lost paradise through the temptations of the devil. In consuming the forbidden fruit, what were they doing but searching for something better than what they had already?

It is this pernicious but alluring tendency to seek incessantly to obtain something better—a form of restless ambition and discontent—which resulted in the fall of the angels. Never forget the fall of those angels, and never forget the expulsion of Adam and Eve from the garden of paradise! For these two primordial examples illustrate the perils which result from seeking always for something new and better.

Recall also the example of Lot from the pages of holy Scriptures. He had shown himself firmly committed to holiness while he was surrounded by sinners in the city of Sodom. But after he went wandering in the wilderness, vainly seeking after safety, he sank into the very depths of shame and was drunkenly induced to commit incest with his own daughters.[62]

There is also another kind of wandering or instability which I should warn you about. This is when a religious remains physically present in his monastery or convent where he is committed by his vows; yet he permits his heart and mind to go far astray. Often this happens when he becomes overly engrossed in secular affairs, even those which are useful and necessary to his community. One must guard one's self diligently against this hidden peril! For many religious people are compelled for quite legitimate reasons to involve themselves in the business of the world, yet this can very soon become a snare which draws them away from stability in their spiritual vocation. The apostle Paul speaks of this peril when he says, "No one fighting for God should allow himself to be entangled in the affairs of this world."[63]

The best guard against this peril is to follow another counsel of Saint Paul, namely, "Pray without ceasing!"[64]

---

[62] See Genesis 19.

[63] 2 Timothy 2:4.

[64] 1 Thessalonians 5:16.

For constant internal prayer keeps one's heart firmly fixed on God, even in the midst of other activities. Thus it protects the most valuable form of stability there is—namely, spiritual stability. When spiritual stability has been fully cultivated, there will no longer arise any of that restless discontentment which gives rise to the desire to wander about from place to place.

O Soul, strive earnestly after this spiritual stability, for it is the secret to possessing peace and tranquility wherever you may be.

14

Despair Is Banished
by Faithful Hope

After Dissolute Wandering has wandered off, an even gloomier character arrives: the vice of Despair. Despair seems to be utterly devoid of personality and energy, and stares blankly at the ground. Its abjection is so profound that it can be expressed neither by tears nor by sighs. Like Worldly Melancholy, Despair is clad entirely in black. But whereas Melancholy possessed a certain style, even to the point of vanity, Despair seems to lack both form and substance. In barely audible tones which resemble the hissing of a serpent, it speaks to the soul thus:

O wretched Soul, how many and how serious are the sins you have committed! How innumerable are your acts of negligence! You claim to be religious, and yet you have not changed yourself, or your way of life, for the better in the slightest. You cannot name a single fault of yours which you have *really* corrected, or a single vice which you have fully overcome and successfully eradicated. All your striving has been futile and shall continue to be futile.

Wickedness, weakness, and slackness have become unbreakable habits for you. Each time you strive to raise yourself up, you end up slipping, and often ending up worse than what you were before!

Unending punishment for all your past misdeeds inevitably awaits you, and long experience has shown you that you are incapable of amending yourself. So why even bother to try? Why give up the few joys and pleasures you have in this passing life since you really don't have much chance at all of obtaining the eternal happiness of heaven. Seize the pleasures of this earthly day, give in to temptation since, even if you try to resist, in the end you're sure to fail!

As this discourse reaches its conclusion, Faithful Hope enters the scene. He is clad in gleaming armor and holds a shield bearing the inscription "Fides" (Faith) and has in his right hand a golden sword with the words "Verbum Dei" (The Word of God) written in silver upon the hilt. As soon as he arrives, Despair begins to shrink and fade away visibly. In a confident and resonant voice, Faithful Hope speaks thus to the soul:

O blessed Soul, recall that you are redeemed by the blood of the Son of God, who has pledged forgiveness for all those who repent!

If you are anxious about your previous crimes and sins, think for a moment about some well-known and instructive examples from Sacred Scripture. Take King David—he was both a murderer and an adulterer. Yet the Lord not only forgave him but bestowed upon him special royal dignities and prophetic privileges. Have you not read the psalm in which David proclaims, "I was liberated from the very jaws of hell by the Lord's mercy!"

And consider also the case of Manasseh. This ancient king of Judah was deservedly ranked among the filthiest, most evil, and depraved of all sinners. Nevertheless, through repentance and penance, he escaped eternal death and damnation, and his life was preserved through the infinite mercy of God.[65]

Call to mind next the beautiful Mary Magdalene. She was a notorious sinner, a courtesan tainted with the stain of countless acts of fornication. But she hurled herself at the sacred feet of Jesus, the font of heaven's mercy. And she washed His holy feet with the tears of sincere penitence, wiping them dry lovingly with her silken and delicate hair. She covered these divine feet with kisses of passionate devotion and anointed Him with the rarest and most precious of anointments. And because of this, she who had been a sinner, a fornicator, became a beloved companion of the Lord—the first to witness the radiant glory of His

---

[65] See 2 Chronicles 33.

resurrection, the first to embrace His risen body, the first to announce His triumph over death, the "apostle of the apostles." *She* did not succumb to despair over her sins, which were surely greater than yours. Let her faith and hope be an example to you whenever you feel discouraged!

Even Saint Peter himself, the Prince of Apostles, sinned most terribly in his cowardly threefold denial of the Lord. Yet, by his threefold confession of love, he was released from all his guilt and shame. And Saint Paul, under his former name of Saul, had been a vicious and relentless persecutor of the Church. Yet out of this, he was transformed into an apostle and made the chosen vessel of the Gospel of salvation.

O Soul, if you consider all these cases of repentant sinners, why should you listen to the malignant and mephitic musings of Despair? It is not possible that your sins are greater than those enumerated above. Yet all of these persons were not only forgiven but ascended to the very heights of sanctity.

And the Lord is on your side in all of this. He has His arms open to forgive you freely and completely the moment you repent. For truly it is written, "Whenever a sinner weeps over his guilt, he shall be immediately forgiven."[66] And again, we read, "The Lord says, 'I desire not the death of the wicked.'"[67]

---

[66] Ezekiel 18:21.
[67] Ezekiel 33:11.

And regarding your apparent failure to reform your behavior in the past, I have only this to say: if today you earnestly desire to change yourself, then today you *can* change yourself! Do not put off till tomorrow what you can easily do today. Our actions are all the result of our own will, and nothing else. Everything which we do, we do because we *want* to do it. Therefore, a person who does not cease to sin does not actually really *want* to cease to sin. But a person who genuinely wishes to abstain from sin, will abstain from sin. Our volition, and therefore our actions, are, by their very nature, always within our own control.

For this reason, as long as you truly desire to be saved, you can be saved. As long as you truly desire to be saved, you *will* be saved. So hearken not to the evil voice of Despair, but rather, be strong in faith and courageous in hope!

15

AVARICE IS CORRECTED
BY DETACHMENT

NEXT, AVARICE APPEARS. He is dressed in quite shabby, cheap clothing, but his pockets are stuffed with gold coins. His expression is one of voracious, wolf-like hunger, and his eyes shift around with greedy restlessness. In an anxious and nervous manner, he speaks thus to the soul:

O Soul, you live in the world, and so you are obliged to make use of, and to possess, the things of the world. You are not yet a pure spirit, and therefore you cannot exist without the support of material things.

It is certainly no sin for you to acquire the resources you legitimately need and desire. It is not as if you were seeking to possess all the gold of the Orient, or all the treasures of the sea, or trying to rival Solomon in his wealth and splendor! No, you just want what is necessary to make yourself comfortable and secure.

And it's certain that if you don't do this, there are plenty of other people who will seize whatever you don't grasp. And they will undoubtedly make poor use of these resources. But *your* intentions are all good, and so whatever you can acquire will be directed to a commendable and upright purpose.

Detachment from the World, the virtue opposed to Avarice, is also present. He wears neat but simple attire and has a calm and peaceful manner. In a gentle and kindly voice, he replies:

You should realize, my friend, that the things of this world—money, treasures, and property—are seldom obtained without sin and struggle, and that they are retained and managed only with anxiety and tribulation. Indeed, it is the nature of this fallen and corrupt world that its riches are seldom bestowed without moral compromise.

And if you observe those who succeed in acquiring the things of this world in abundance, what do you see? Are they ever really content with what they have? No, definitely not! For the more one possesses, the more one desires to possess. Thus it is written in the Scriptures, "The greedy person is never satisfied with his wealth."[68] Avarice is, by its very nature, insatiable—the more you feed this hungry monster, the larger and more voracious it grows!

---

[68] Ecclesiastes 5:9.

Saint Paul condemns avarice in striking terms, telling us that "greed is a form of idolatry."[69] In another place, he expounds further on this, saying, "Whoever desires to become rich falls into the temptations and the snares of the devil, and immerses himself in countless perilous desires. Whoever becomes enmeshed in these becomes submerged in destruction and perdition!"[70]

The apostle Saint James likewise highlights the grave moral perils of riches and the pursuit of riches. "All you who are rich," he exclaims, "mourn and weep for the miseries which await you! For your riches are rotting away, like garments which are consumed by the worm. Your gold and your silver shall be consumed by rust, and this rust shall stand as a witness against you, and will consume your flesh like a burning fire!"[71]

And Our Lord Himself spoke frequently of the evils of cupidity and avarice, warning emphatically of its insidious perils to the soul. For He indeed once said, "It is difficult for one who possess riches to gain admittance to the kingdom of heaven." Using an apt and illustrative similitude, He went on to declare, "It is easier for a camel to pass through the eye of a needle than for a rich person to enter the kingdom of heaven!"[72]

---

[69] Ephesians 5:5.

[70] 1 Timothy 6:9.

[71] James 5:1–3.

[72] Matthew 19:24.

If the desire for riches is dangerous for people in secular life, how much more hazardous is it for those who have committed themselves to a life of religious conversion! For they have undertaken to renounce the world and all earthly riches, to emulate the holy poverty of Our Lord Jesus Christ. For such persons who have committed themselves to embracing simplicity of life and detachment from the world for the sake of God, the following words of the Gospel may be understood to apply in a particularly pertinent way: "Do not be anxious about tomorrow, or what you will eat or drink, or how you shall clothe yourself! Rather, seek first the kingdom of God and its justice, and all these things shall be provided for you."[73]

O how wonderful, how wise, how comforting is this divine utterance! For there is no one who is more secure in this life than the person who desires to possess nothing except for Christ. For in having Christ, everything which is truly necessary is also attained. Thus it was that Saint Paul was poor in earthly goods but felt himself to be rich beyond all comparison, describing himself as "having nothing, but possessing everything."[74] He shunned everything that was superfluous and contented himself with the bare necessities of life, saying, "Having food and clothing, let us be content with these."[75]

---

[73] Matthew 6:25, 33.

[74] 2 Corinthians 6:10.

[75] 1 Timothy 6:8.

Consider, O Soul, how do riches and abundance of goods really profit a person? Even during this life, acquiring them is a source of toil and labor, retaining them is a source of anxiety and worry, and losing them is a source of grief and loss. And where does the rich person end up? In precisely the same place as the pauper—he is equally afflicted with old age, infirmity, and, in due course, death. The grave is the final resting place for both! What, therefore, is the benefit of being rich?

O Soul, remember that "we come into this world naked, and we depart from it naked."[76] "We take nothing into this world, nor are we able to take anything out of it!"[77]

---

[76] Job 1:21.
[77] Ecclesiastes 5:15.

16

STINGINESS IS REBUKED
BY GENEROSITY

NEXT, THE VICE of Stinginess appears on the scene—a gaunt and miserly character, with a miserable and mean demeanor, a pallid complexion, and thin and tightly pursed lips. In a harsh and severe voice, it says to the soul:

O foolish and gullible Soul, beware of being too openhanded! If you give away too much to the poor and the needy, you may not have sufficient left over to fulfill your own proper responsibilities. You have yourself and your family to take care of! You must think of these first. If there's anything left over, then (and only then) maybe think about giving to the poor—but not until you are first absolutely secure of your own financial security, if and when that ever happens!

The virtue of Generosity, who displays a healthy, ruddy complexion and an open and amicable expression, responds as follows:

O Soul, if you faithfully follow the example of the apostle Saint Paul, you will be able both to give generously and freely to the poor *and* to be confident that you will always have enough for yourself and for those for whom you are immediately responsible. For he wisely wrote, "If you heart is willing, it is acceptable to give out of what you have, not out of what you *don't* have. Use your own abundance to provide for the poverty of others. Then it may well come to pass that out of the abundance of others your own poverty will be provided for!"[78]

For God will certainly never abandon those who give for love of Him, nor withhold His generosity and providence towards them. Indeed, it is seldom that we see a generous giver fall upon hard times himself; more often, we see him blessed with even more prosperity and happiness! For "the Lord loves a cheerful giver," and "the one who sows bountifully will reap bountifully."[79]

Jesus Christ, the incarnate Truth, clearly exhorted us to be free and generous in our giving when He said, "Whatever is surplus to your own needs, give freely as alms! And, behold, all things shall become pure for you."[80]

Call to mind, O Soul, the parable in the Gospel of the rich man and the pauper, Lazarus, who sat at his gate. Now,

---

[78] 2 Corinthians 8:12–14.
[79] 2 Corinthians 9:7.
[80] Luke 11:41.

the rich man was damned eternally. Why? Not because he actually took the property of others but because he clung too tenaciously to his own property and turned a blind eye to the needs of others. For to deny or ignore the needs of the poor is to deny or ignore Christ Himself, who is truly present "even in the least of His brethren." And what does Our Lord say to those who deny Him in this manner? It is to them that He utters those most dreaded and ominous words: "Depart from Me, O you accursed, into the eternal fire prepared for the devil and his angels. For I was hungry, and you gave Me nothing to eat."[81]

---

[81] Matthew 25:41–42.

THE TEMPTATIONS OF THEFT AND FRAUD ARE DISPELLED BY INNOCENCE

THEFT AND FRAUD then approach the Soul. They are part-ners and companions—brother and sister, in fact. Both move almost silently and with furtive caution. Theft, the brother, speaks first, saying:

If you do not take from the property of others, you will simply not be able to survive! Life has not dealt you your fair share. You do not have as much as you need and de-serve, but plenty of others have more than enough. This is simply not just, but merely the actions of blind fate and random chance. It is up to *you* to correct things! Take what you can, and so restore the balance which justice demands. O Soul, if you do not help yourself, no one else is going to help you!

To this, Fraud, his sister, then adds, speaking in a sneaky whisper:

O Soul, you have been entrusted with a lot of resources and money, and have been given also a *lot* of hard work and responsibilities. As long as you do your job and take care of what is entrusted to you well, what harm is there if you secretly appropriate a little for yourself? After all, *you* are the one doing the work.

And no one really gets hurt. Go ahead and take a little for yourself! It won't make any real difference in the big picture, but it will help *you* a lot—and not yourself only, but also your loved ones. It's just a drop in the bucket for them, and no one could reasonably deny you the right to put a little aside for yourself. Why, even Scripture virtually says as much! For it is written, "Do not muzzle an ox while it treads the grain."[82]

Innocence is also present. This virtue, Innocence, has the appearance of a young child, yet there is deep wisdom in her eyes. She responds gently to the temptations of both Fraud and Deception, speaking thus:

O Soul, it is infinitely better to suffer poverty and want, and to be entirely unable to support others (or even oneself), than to consent to these heinous temptations of Theft

---

[82] Deuteronomy 25:4.

and Fraud! For to seize the property of others is to lock the entrance of the kingdom of heaven!

For acts of theft and fraud are a rebellion against the order and justice established by both God and humankind. They reflect the valuing of the goods of this passing world above the justice of heaven, and show a patent mistrust in the providence and wisdom of the Lord.

It is true that the person who steals or practices fraud may gain something in this world's riches, but he bargains away the integrity of the soul to do so. And Saint Paul tells us, "Neither thieves nor brigands shall attain the kingdom of God."[83] What is there which is more valuable than this eternal and infinite kingdom? Even all the gold of the earth, even the rarest of pearls and the most magnificent of jewels are nothing in comparison to it!

Trust in the providence of God to take care of you. Seek first the kingdom of heaven and its justice, and all that you need shall be provided to you.[84] God has promised it, and God will surely deliver upon His word!

---

[83] 1 Corinthians 6:10.
[84] Matthew 6:33.

18

CONCEALMENT AND DECEPTION ARE REPRIMANDED BY TRUTHFULNESS

Next, Concealment and Deception arrive on the scene. Like Theft and Fraud, they are both evidently shifty characters. But the distinctive feature of this pair is that each of them has two faces—one on the back of their heads and one on the front. Sometimes these faces match, but more often they reflect quite different expressions and sentiments. For this reason, it is very difficult to determine which one is genuine and which one is fake.

It is Concealment who speaks first to the soul, saying:

O Soul, I offer you one single piece of advice, and it is wise and useful. You are *not* obliged to give the whole truth to everyone all the time. For example, if someone asks you to do something for him, or to give him something, simply say to him, "I'm so sorry, but I'm not able to help you!" It's not exactly a lie, because it's no one's business but yours, and no one but you really knows what you can and cannot do.

You don't owe anyone else any explanation for your decisions and actions. Protect your privacy—tell people as much or as little as you please. To remain silent about the truth is *not* to lie; sometimes, remaining silent and keeping things to yourself is simply to practice common sense and discretion.

Tell the truth, but be selective. Tell only as much or as little as suits you!

To this, Deception adds:

What my friend Concealment has to say is all well and good, and sound advice. But why stop there? Does it really make any difference if you conceal the truth, or tell a little white lie? Sometimes this is extremely helpful and expedient, and it's always harmless.

For example, someone might ask you to help him out in some way. My good friend Concealment would probably advise you to reply, "Sorry, I'm not able to do anything for you at the moment." But what if the person making the requests persists and asks you, "Why not?" O Soul, what are you going to say then—"Because I don't really want to"? I think not! No, you're going to have to make something up, use a little creative fiction. And what's the harm in that? It protects *his* feelings, and it protects *your* appearance. It's good for everyone involved.

The virtue Truthfulness also happens to be present and does not hesitate to respond to the temptations of these two vices and their specious persuasions. With a frank and open expression, this virtue responds:

No one can lie to God! If you try to deceive others, you may succeed for a time. But you will inevitably end up ensnaring yourself in your own lies.

O Soul, each time you lie or deceive anyone, you compromise your integrity and damage and deform your own nature. For Scripture declares to us that "the lying mouth kills the soul."[85] And we are gravely warned, "Deceitful mouths are destined for the pit of burning fire and brimstone."[86]

Don't listen to the advice of Concealment and Deception—for by their very nature, they are liars. Why should you give credit to anything they say? When you betray the truth, you betray Christ, who is the Truth itself. And, more than this, you betray yourself!

---

[85] Wisdom 1:11.
[86] Revelation 21:8.

19

GLUTTONY IS RESTRAINED
BY MODERATION

THE VICE OF Gluttony then appears. His nature is very easy to recognize, for he is immensely fat. His face is framed by a triple chin, and his abdomen hangs over his belt. He breathes in a heavy and labored manner, and he sweats profusely. Remnants of food are visible on his clothing and countenance. He speaks thus to the soul:

O Soul, remember that it was God Himself who very graciously bestowed upon humankind the wonderful and magnificent gift of food! Moreover, He emphatically declared *all* foods to be clean, and to be freely consumed, as we read both in the Gospel and the Acts of the Apostles. Therefore, whosoever refuses this gift, or accepts it only stingily, is treating this great and holy offering with impious disdain!

Let us, therefore, partake freely and without reserve. Eat and drink to your fill, my friend, for it is a gift from the Most High!

The virtue of Moderation arrives just as Gluttony concludes his speech. He is lean and light but muscular and healthy. His bearing and demeanor embody energy and strength. Speaking thus, he intelligently refutes Gluttony's foolish advice:

O Gluttony, what you say is true, but only *partially* so. For God did indeed create food for human consumption, and He did declare all foods to be clean. But food serves the purpose of nourishing the body and sustaining life and should be used according to this purpose.

To exceed proper measure in anything, even a good thing, is a vice. And Scripture repeatedly warns us of the dangers and sinfulness of gluttony, which is nothing other than the consuming of anything beyond its proper measure.

Consider the cases of Sodom, which was obliterated by the infallible justice of the Lord. Now, amongst its numerous crimes and abominations, gluttony was counted as one of them. For we read in the prophet Ezekiel: "This was the iniquity of Sodom: pride, and stuffing themselves with food and excess, and sloth."[87]

---

[87] Ezekiel 16:49.

To consume food with proper order and measure, one should approach it as a sick person takes his prescribed medicine. For a person who is ill takes what he needs of the appropriate medicine for the sake of his health and nothing more. He certainly does not seek to derive pleasure and gratification from it! Food, like medicine, if taken without measure and without regard to its proper purpose, ceases to be healthful and becomes harmful.

This does not mean, of course, that there may not be *any* pleasure at all in eating and drinking. But such pleasure is merely incidental to the objective of sustaining health, and not to be pursued as a goal in itself. Indeed, proper moderation actually serves to enhance one's enjoyment in consuming God's gifts of nourishment.

We hear our Savior Himself giving a clear and unequivocal admonition about the sin of overindulgence. "Beware," He warns, "that your hearts are not rendered heavy with gluttony and drunkenness!"[88] The apostle Saint Paul also reprimands those who make "the stomach their god."[89] He reminds us that "food is made for the stomach, and the stomach made for food. And God shall do away with both!"[90] In saying this, he is saying that food serves the purpose of physical nourishment and sustenance in this

---

[88] Luke 21:34.
[89] Philippians 3:19.
[90] 1 Corinthians 6:13.

present world rather than gratification. We should eat to live, not live to eat!

The virtue of moderation has been developed to maturity in those who eat to the point of sufficiency, not to complete satiety. Such people always leave the table still a little hungry rather than completely full. Another reliable sign of the presence of this virtue is when a person does not choose his food on the basis of what brings him sensory gratification but rather on the basis of what fulfills the needs of the body. Such a person will typically prefer simplicity over luxury, and what is natural and common over what is exotic and expensive.

O Soul, this is a good and salubrious practice, beneficial to the health of both the body and the soul!

20

INANE ELATION IS
BROUGHT UNDER CONTROL
BY HOLY SORROW

INANE ELATION THEN appears before the soul. She is giggling foolishly and behaves like a person who is slightly intoxicated. She says to the soul:

O Soul, why keep your joy and amusement concealed within your heart? Show it to the world! Grin, laugh aloud, dance a jig!

You should let everyone know what it is that is the source of your mirth so that they may share it. For joy is contagious: if you display your own amusement, others will also be amused.

Holy Sorrow also happens to be present. He is quite unlike either Worldly Melancholy or Despair, because, although serious, he has a certain underlying security and strength. With gravity and wisdom, he responds thus:

O Soul, I acknowledge this advice is not *entirely* bad or false. But first consider carefully: What is it that has caused your mirth and elation? Is it success or prosperity in some worldly, passing thing? Is it that your pride or your physical senses have been gratified? Is it in something which could cause embarrassment or discomfort to another? Is it mockery of another human being? Would your laughter cause pain to the ears of one of your brothers or sisters?

And before surrendering yourself to empty mirth, ask yourself the following questions: Have you yet succeeded in conquering the devil? Are you *really* sure that you will escape the fires of hell? Have you completed your earthly exile in this valley of tears, and do you already enjoy your heavenly homeland?

Or perhaps you have forgotten the words of our Savior, who declared, "The world will rejoice, but you shall mourn. But your sadness will be transformed into joy."[91] Or possibly some other, even more emphatic words have slipped from your memory—namely, when Christ said, "Alas for you who laugh now, for you shall mourn and weep!"[92] And the converse of this is also articulated in the Gospel: "Blessed are those who mourn, for they will be consoled."[93]

---

[91] John 16:20.
[92] Luke 6:25.
[93] Matthew 5:4.

O Soul, do not, therefore, give yourself over to inane elation and mindless joy; for your battle is not yet over, and your exile here is not yet complete. You have not yet achieved your goal or arrived at your heavenly destination, nor can you be assured that you have escaped eternal damnation.

Consider the case of a person held in a human prison, in a state of confinement and deprivation, and still anxiously awaiting his final sentence. Now, if such a person were to give himself over to unrestrained laughter and flippancy, would you not consider him to be quite insane? Indeed you would, and rightly so! But is not your situation during this mortal life a lot like theirs?

21

GARRULITY IS SILENCED
BY PRUDENT RESTRAINT

NEXT, THE VICE of Garrulity, or excessive talkativeness, arrives on the scene. Its nature is readily recognized, for an almost uninterrupted stream of words issues from its mouth. Even when no one is present to listen, it seems to have difficulty in stopping this incessant speech. After a long and wordy greeting and introduction, Garrulity addresses the soul thus:

The person who speaks his mind freely is not guilty of any crime or sin, as long as he says good and edifying things. It is only the person who says *wicked* things, even if he speaks little, who may be regarded as culpable.

O Soul, *you* certainly do not intend to say wicked things! So, therefore, speak freely. Say as much as you please, to whomsoever you please! For, as long as you do not deliberately speak any evil, there is no sin in this whatsoever.

But Prudent Restraint is present also. He seems to be listening attentively to all that is being said and reflecting carefully upon it. After a lengthy pause, in which he is evidently weighing each of his words, he says to the soul:

What has been said is, in principle, quite true. But while there are many things which are said which *seem* to be good and innocent, in practice they lead to some evil or sin. Sacred Scripture points this out to us by declaring, "In much speaking, you will not avoid sin."[94]

It is true that in much speaking, you may actually avoid saying anything intentionally wicked or criminal. But will you avoid saying something which is idle, useless, or simply a waste of time and words? That is hardly possible! And does not Our Lord state that we shall be called upon to give a full account of every such idle word which we have spoken? For the Gospel says, "Everyone will have to give account on the Day of Judgment for every empty word they have spoken."[95] But who can possibly avoid empty, inane, and pointless words in a long conversation?

O Soul, it behooves you to preserve appropriate measure and reserve in your speech. Avoid useless words altogether! Before opening your mouth, make it a habit to ask yourself, "Will these words serve any good and holy purpose?"

---

[94] Proverbs 10.
[95] Matthew 12:36.

And even if you answer in the affirmative, sometimes it is still more prudent to remain silent. For King David himself wrote, "I was humble, and remained silent even from good things."[96] By saying this, he demonstrates how immensely valuable a thing is silence, since it is sometimes to be chosen in preference to other good possibilities. Sometimes, O Soul, silence is better than wise advice; sometimes it is better even than a kindly word!

---

[96] Psalms 38.

22

Fleshly Desire and Lust Are Put to Flight by Carnal Purity and Chastity

Fleshly Desire and Lust then make an entrance. As first glance, Fleshly Desire has the appearance of a young woman; however, a more careful look reveals that she is closer to middle age but dressed in a fashion more befitting a much younger person. She is wearing a very short skirt and excessive makeup, and she moves her hips as she walks in a manner which is evidently intended to be seductive. Lust, her companion, is there also. He has greasy black hair, a long goat-like beard, and a waxed moustache, with a showy golden chain hanging around his neck. A leering, wolf-like glint shines forth from his beady eyes.

Fleshly Desire speaks to the soul first, saying:

Surely, it is no very serious or wicked thing for males and females to do what their impulses prompt them to do? For we all have desires and urges of the flesh, and somehow or the other, we must obtain satisfaction—either with others or by our own devices. What on earth is wrong with that?

But Purity and Chastity are also present. Purity is a young man wearing a crisp white shirt and with a clean-cut appearance. Chastity is a young, blue-eyed woman. She is dressed modestly but elegantly, and she projects confidence and assurance. Both of these virtues, though apparently unpreoccupied with their appearance, are undeniably much more attractive than Fleshly Desire or Lust.

Purity's response to the temptations of Fleshly Desire is in the following terms:

Our physical impulses may sometimes be legitimately followed, but only in the way and for the purposes for which God and nature established them. Anything which deviates from that is an abuse of oneself and of others, and leads to the sin of impurity. And such impurity, according to the apostle Saint Paul, is something which separates us from God. For he reminds us that "the impure will never possess the kingdom of God!"[97]

However, Lust is quick to respond, and adds:

O Soul, why do you resist the allurement of carnal pleasure? For you do not know what is to come after you, and

---

[97] 1 Corinthians 6.

you do not really know for sure whether there is any future life at all. Seize the day which has been given to you, and enjoy things as much as you possibly can! If God did not wish us to desire the pleasures of the flesh and to indulge our lust, then why did He create human beings as males and females?

Upon hearing this specious argument, Chastity addresses the soul thus:

Do not be oblivious, my friend, to the fact that there *is* a life which follows this one, and that we shall all face judgment for our actions performed in the here and now! If you live in the present world in a chaste and holy manner, then you will rejoice for all eternity. But if you now indulge in the brief and passing pleasures of lust and sin, then you will suffer in the unquenchable fires of hell forever and ever! Hence it much wiser to choose the path of chastity than to sink into the foul mire fornication. My sworn foe, the vice of Lust, has himself just admitted that we do not know how long we are to live here, nor did we know what will confront us afterwards!

It is, of course, true what he says—that God created human beings as male and female, and that the union of male and female is part of God's plan for humanity and for creation. And permission to marry, with the blessing of God, is granted to human beings, as well as the right to choose not to do so, with vows of consecrated celibacy. To people who are called to this second way of life, permission is *not* granted to seek fleshly union with another.

But for anyone, whether he is called to marriage or celibacy for the sake of the kingdom of God, fornication is not permitted. And it will never go unpunished. Have you never read the words of the apostle, or do you think that they may be safely ignored? For he writes, "Flee from fornication, my brothers and sisters! Whatever other sins people may commit, they are committed outside the body. But anyone who commits fornication sins against his own body."[98]

If you think this admonition is not worth taking any notice of, then later on Saint Paul gives an even more stern and striking warning, telling us that the sins of the flesh shall lead to nothing but eternal misery and regret. "Neither adulterers," he declares, "nor fornicators, nor perverts will inherit the kingdom of God."[99]

O how brief is the pleasure of fornication, that for the sake of this momentary delight, one should lose the eternal glory and infinite bliss of heaven! What lasting good does it do for the body, or soul, or mind, and what profit does it really bring anyone? It brings no lasting or substantial happiness, but only misery and heartbreak in this life, and unending regret and pain in the blazing and unquenchable fires of hell which will follow!

---

[98] 1 Corinthians 6:18.

[99] 1 Corinthians 6:9.

SPIRITUAL FORNICATION IS CORRECTED BY PURITY OF HEART

THE VICE OF Spiritual Fornication arrives on the scene next. Unlike Fleshly Desire and Lust, the true character of Spiritual Fornication is not immediately manifest in his appearance. He is dressed in a non-descript and slovenly manner, with a pale and flaccid countenance. In a feeble and somewhat effeminate voice, he speaks thus to the soul:

O Soul, you cannot be held culpable for the thoughts which spontaneously arise in your mind, nor the desires which naturally arise in your heart. For these are your own business and do not hurt anyone else. They never amount to any actions or deeds and so cannot be regarded as sins.

But Purity of Heart, the virtue opposed to Spiritual Fornication, soon follows. He is tall and broad shouldered, with a healthy glow beaming forth from his honest and noble face. He overhears what Spiritual Fornication has been saying to the soul. In his turn, he then begins to speak:

O Soul, the person does indeed sin who commits fornication within his heart. For did not Our Lord Himself assert in the Gospel, "Whoever looks upon a woman for the purpose of lust has committed fornication with her in his heart"?[100] And we find a similar principle articulated in the book of Job, in which it is written, "I made a pact with my eye, that I should not stare at any maiden."[101]

For God perceives not only our external actions but also the thoughts of our minds and the movements of our hearts. Can we be wholly pleasing to our Creator, who sees both the interior and exterior, if we cultivate lustful thoughts and desires in our hearts and contemplate the performance of illicit acts? Certainly not! Hence it is that through the prophet Isaiah, God admonishes us, "Remove your wicked cogitations from my sight!" And Saint Paul likewise testifies, "Upon the day on which God shall judge the hidden secrets of each person, our thoughts and desires shall arise as witnesses against us."[102]

[This is not to say that every instinct of attraction to a member of the opposite sex is sinful in itself. Far from it!

---

[100] Matthew 5:28.
[101] Job 31:1.
[102] Romans 2:16.

For they are a normal and natural part of the God-given gift of gender, and necessary for the continuation of the human race and the establishment of Christian families. Nevertheless, the deliberate cultivation of these thoughts as a source of gratification, or the misdirection of them to unnatural purposes, can become the "fornication committed in the heart," which is so sternly condemned by Christ. There is a need for wise discretion here![103]]

---

[103] This last paragraph has been added by the translator to the original text to help clarify the distinction between spiritual fornication and normal feelings of sexual attraction.

Worldly Attachment Is Tempered by Longing for Heaven

Once Spiritual Fornication has departed, Worldly Attachment, the last of the vices to be overcome, enters. In some ways, he seems to be a fine character, elegantly dressed and with clear confidence and intelligence in his face. Although his manner and bearing are pleasant, affable, and friendly, there is something vaguely dishonest and shifty about him. He addresses the soul in the following terms:

O Soul, what is there which could be more beautiful, more pleasing, and more delightful than what you find in this present world? How miraculous are the vaults of the skies above us, the glorious radiance of the sun, the shimmering gleam of the moon, and the regular and harmonious course of the innumerable stars!

And what could be more wonderful than this earth, with its verdant forests, its meadows adorned by multicolored flowers, its golden fields of wheat, and its vines laden with sweet and delicious fruits? Behold also the diversity of birds and beasts—the swift steed and fleet-footed hound, the prancing deer and leaping goats, the soaring hawk! Consider also the splendor of the peacock and the subtle sheen of the peaceful turtledove.

And then there are the magnificent works of humanity! Reflect upon the grand palaces and cathedrals rising up to heaven, and the harmony of the organ and dulcet tone of lute and harp. And meditate upon the beauty of humanity itself. How often has your heart been enchanted by the angelic face of some woman or maiden, her shapely figure, her luxurious hair (whether of pure radiant gold or gleaming raven black), her smile which brings joy to your heart, her kiss which makes you forget all your woes in a glorious instant!

Indeed, Soul, this world is truly a wonderful place! You are quite right to love it with all your heart and bind yourself to its good things with all your being and all your yearning.

Once Worldly Attachment has concluded the above discourse, Longing for Heaven appears. She is of an indescribable, otherworldly beauty, with hair color of the rising sun and eyes of the pure, crystalline azure of a summer's sky. Her voice has all the sweetness of celestial harmony and the piquant melodiousness of the nightingale. Though apparently very young, she seems to speak with the wisdom of one who has witnessed countless eons of time and come to know all that human wisdom may know. Thus she speaks to the soul in a resonant musical tone of mellifluous grace:

O Soul, if these things which exist under heaven delight you so much and if you find so much beauty here, how much indescribably vaster will be the delights and beauties of heaven itself? For this world is like a waiting room, or even, at times, a prison. If it is adorned with all the good things you have described, how magnificently and superabundantly must the true city, the true palace—which is heaven itself—surpass everything you have yet seen or even imagined! If the pilgrimage is sometimes pleasant, how stupendously marvelous must the final destination be!

For in this life, we are but mortals, limited and circumscribed in our capacities, perceptions, resources, and freedom. Here, we all bear the yoke of original sin and its manifold and onerous consequences—suffering, sickness, toil, temptation, and, finally, death. How incomparably better is the joy of those who are definitively freed from this burdensome and dolorous yoke of the children of Adam and the progeny of Eve, and whom sorrow and sadness can touch no more, and whom toil and tribulation can no longer so grievously afflict!

O Soul, let your attachment to the things of this world be moderated by the realization that everything here is limited, and all joys and sorrows we experience in this life are merely passing. For there is nothing which comes into existence which will not, soon or later, go out of existence, and nothing is born in this realm of time and space which is not destined eventually to die.

> For here, the rose does blossom,
> And then must fade away,
> And gloom and heavy darkness,
> Must close each passing day.
>
> The sky of gleaming azure
> Must vanish with the night,
> And nighttime's purple grandeur,
> Is crushed by dawn's cold light.
>
> Yea, nothing here is lasting,
> Nothing here endures;
> So set your heart on heaven
> Which lasts forever more.
>
> No eye has seen its beauties,
> No ear has heard its song;
> There every dream is granted,
> For which thy heart does long!

CONCLUSION

O READER, WE have together encountered a multitude of vices and observed the wiles and snares which they typically use to tempt the soul. Moreover, we have heard also how for every vice which assails us, there is a virtue capable of exposing its falsehood and refuting its unwholesome and pernicious urgings. Therefore, it behooves us to cultivate these virtues so that we may be well defended against the multitudinous deceits and nefarious persuasions of the vices. For it is by means of such devices that the wicked devil seeks to launch his attack upon the castle of the soul. But by arming ourselves with these virtues, the soul becomes a veritable fortress—strong, stable, and impregnable!

My beloved Reader, I have written this work for you among my many other occupations by stealing hours away from sleep in the quiet darkness of the night. Hence, I must ask you to forgive any lack of elegance in my writing style. As the work exceeds that customary length of a mere letter, I present it to you as a short book, assigning it the title of *The Battle of the Virtues and Vices*.

If you find anything in this modest and humble tract which provides you with edification, encouragement, or wisdom, then, please, do not hesitate to share it with your brothers and sisters. And may each person who reads this work succeed in conquering every one of the vices and cultivating all the virtues; with the grace and kindly assistance of the one, eternal God—Father, Son, and Holy Spirit—who lives and reigns forever and ever! Amen.[104]

---

[104] The text of the conclusion of the work varies greatly from one manuscript to another. The version offered here draws upon sentiments expressed in several sources.